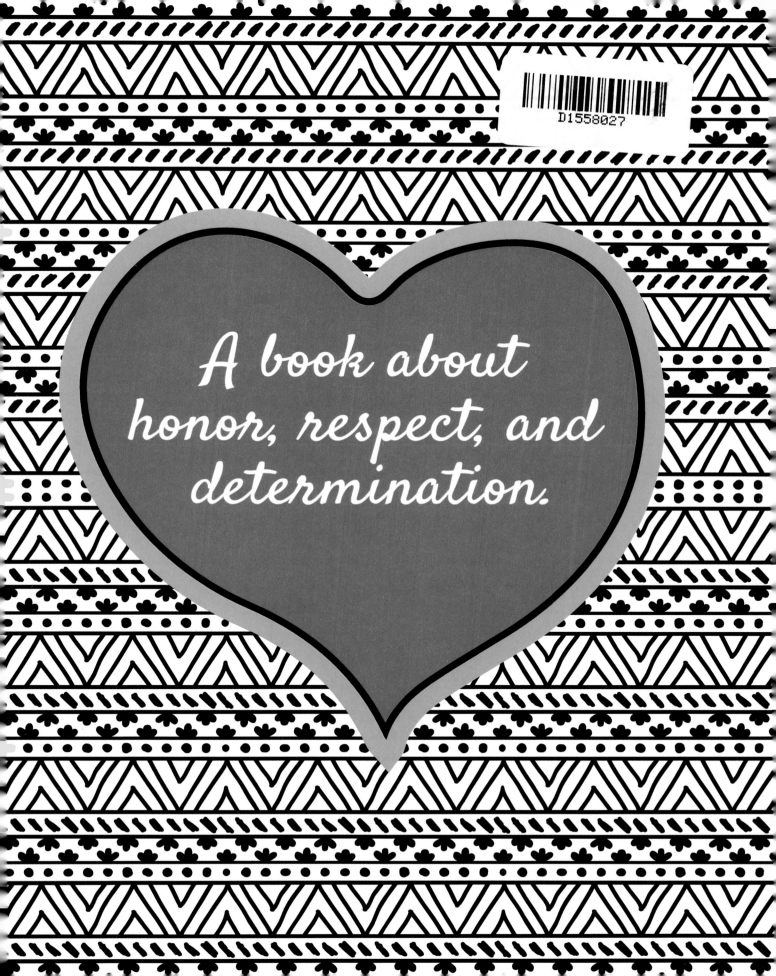

A book about honor, respect, and determination.

This book belongs to:

To my beautiful and amazing daughter,
Nyla Elise Austin.
Thank you for making me better.

My fearless and dedicated parents who
continue to be the wind beneath my wings,
Willie Gordon and Mr. and Mrs. Ronnie and
Barbara Malcom.

My family, aunts, uncles, and cousins all over
the USA.

My tribe of friends who continue to inspire
and encourage me.

This story was birthed from the love and
dedication of the stylist from Divine Perfections
Salon, where the beautiful inside and out,
Barbara Lewis is owner and operator.

This book is dedicated to
Dr. Darryl Lavell Sawyers, your passion and
love for people was pure.
Love is an action word.
You are missed.

Qiana was so excited! School was starting next week and her mother promised that she could get her hair braided for the first day of school.

Qiana spent the entire summer working in her mother's salon. She swept up hair as it was clipped. She washed and folded towels and stacked hair products that her mother's clients would eventually use.

Qiana's mother's salon was a lively place. The walls were painted fire red with pictures of exotic animals and beautiful bold pictures of women in their native West African traditional clothing. The music was loud, lively, and provided a beat that put you right in the center of a traditional West African celebration. You could see the ladies slightly moving their hips as they parted and twisted hair of young and old.

Qiana's mother was originally from West Africa and took pride in her work. Often times, she would spend hours braiding her clients' hair. She spent years perfecting her craft. She was a perfectionist. Qiana's mother Kenya, would proudly take photos of each one of her client's hairstyles. She swirled them around in her styling chair once she was finished. Every customer had a gleaming smile of satisfaction. Qiana's mother was happy when her customers were happy.

The day had come for Qiana to sit in her mother's chair. Qiana spent the night before looking for patterns to make sure her braids were beautiful and original. She learned in her studies that braids had a long, rich history in Africa. In some regions, braids were used to identify regions, kinship, or age. After conducting her research, Qiana grew eager thinking about getting her hair braided.

Qiana's mother called her to the shampoo bowl in the back of the salon. She could smell the aroma of fresh mint all around her as her mother poured the thick shampoo on her scalp. As the warm water flowed through her hair, there was a tingling feeling that rushed all over her head.

Qiana's eyes were closed as she enjoyed this moment with her mother. She thought about the blue skies and warm wind that blew across the African deserts that she read about in her research.

Qiana's mother was very gentle with her as she shampooed her hair. Qiana's mother took a clean towel and softly patted each section of her hair to ensure that the shampoo was rinsed out. Then she was led to the styling chair where a silk cape was drawn around her neck in preparation for the next step.

Next her mother needed to blow dry her hair. She took out her brown blow dryer, plugged it up and lightly swiped each part of her hair to dry it. After drying each section, her mother parted her hair down the middle and sectioned each part off to prepare for the braiding process.

Qiana's mother with confidence and a smile, quietly took each section strand and created a beautiful pattern of twisted hair on Qiana's head. Qiana was tingling with excitement.

After several hours of sitting in her mother's styling chair, her hair was finally finished. Qiana was anxious to see her hair. Her mother whisked her around to the large mirror that sat in the corner of the styling booth and Qiana smiled.

As she looked at her mother's finished work, she could not believe her eyes. Her hair was amazing! It looked just like the picture that she had given her mother. Qiana's mother was smiling.

Qiana was beautiful. She was proud to be able to represent her heritage. She could not wait until the first day of school.

Made in the USA
Middletown, DE
19 June 2021